ALPHABET

ALPHABET

Peter McGough

A

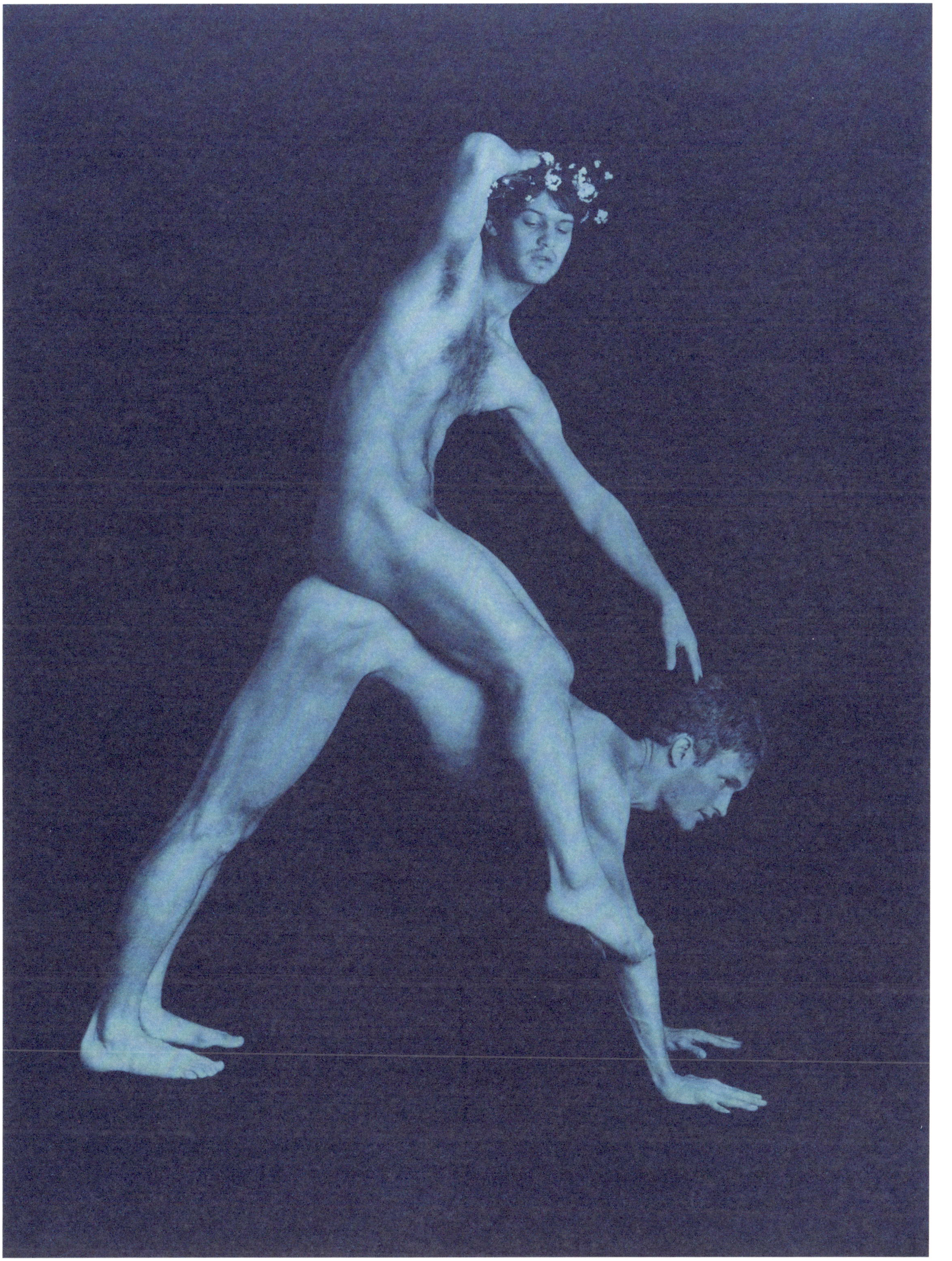

B

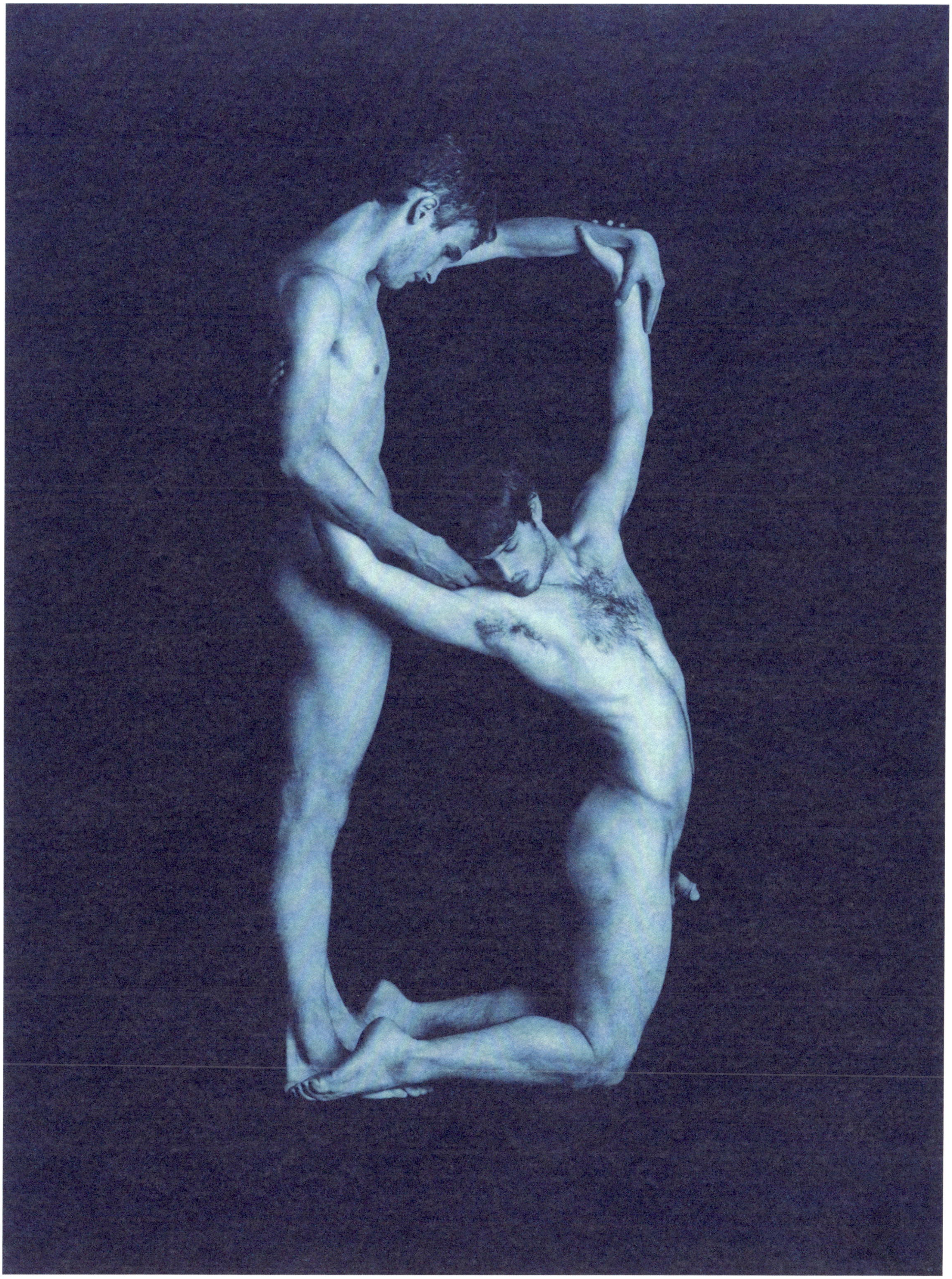

C

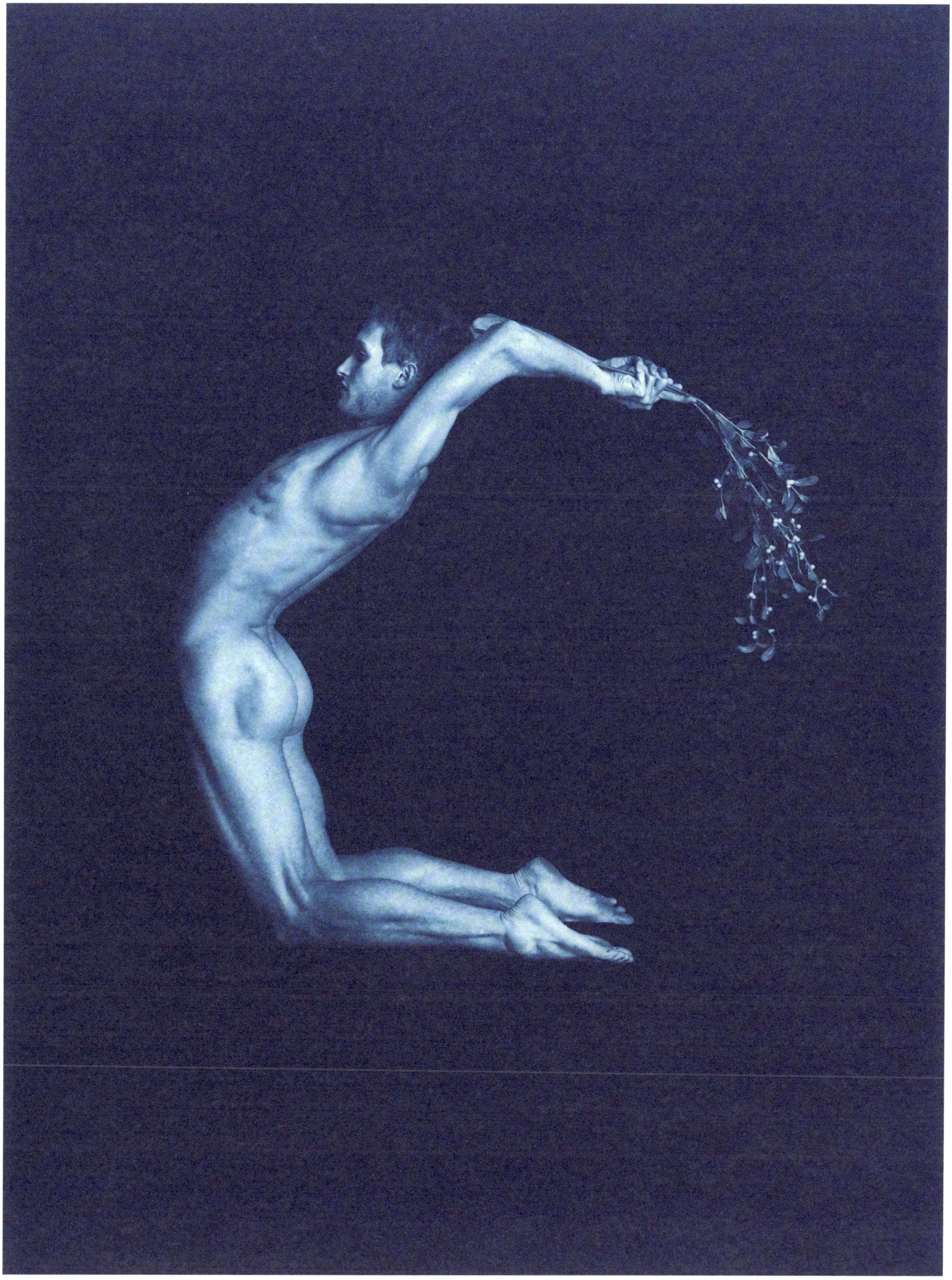

D

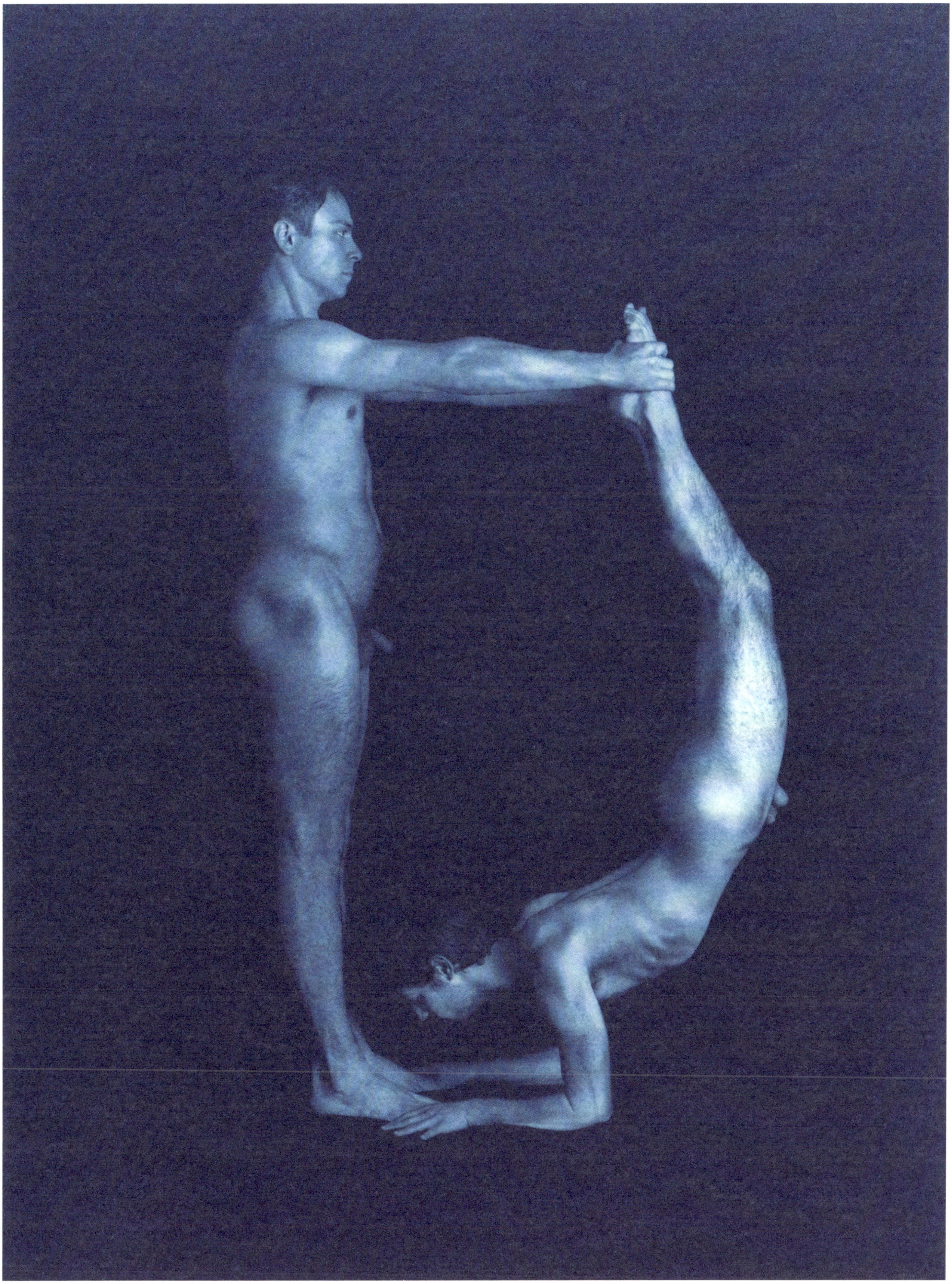

E

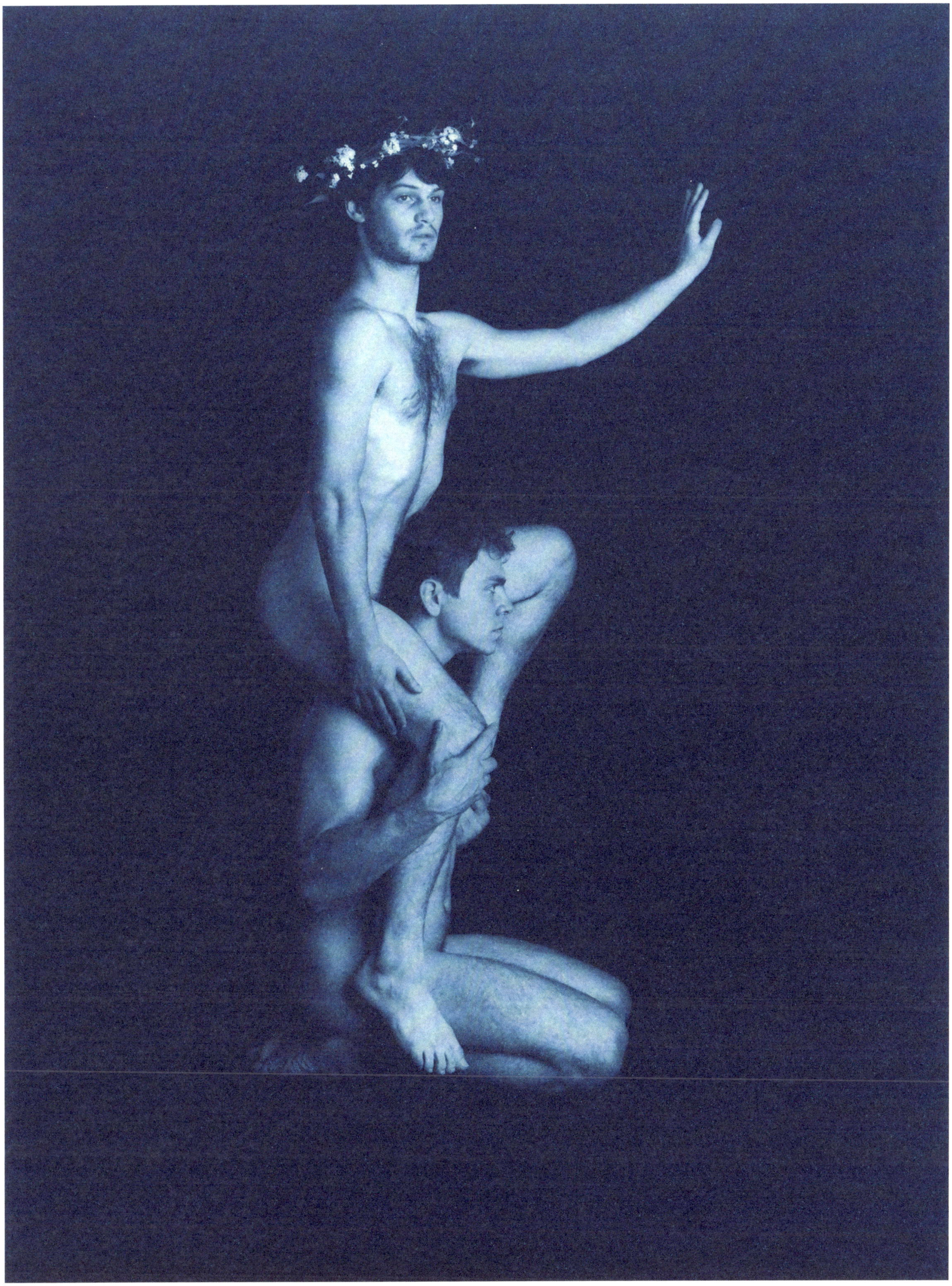

F

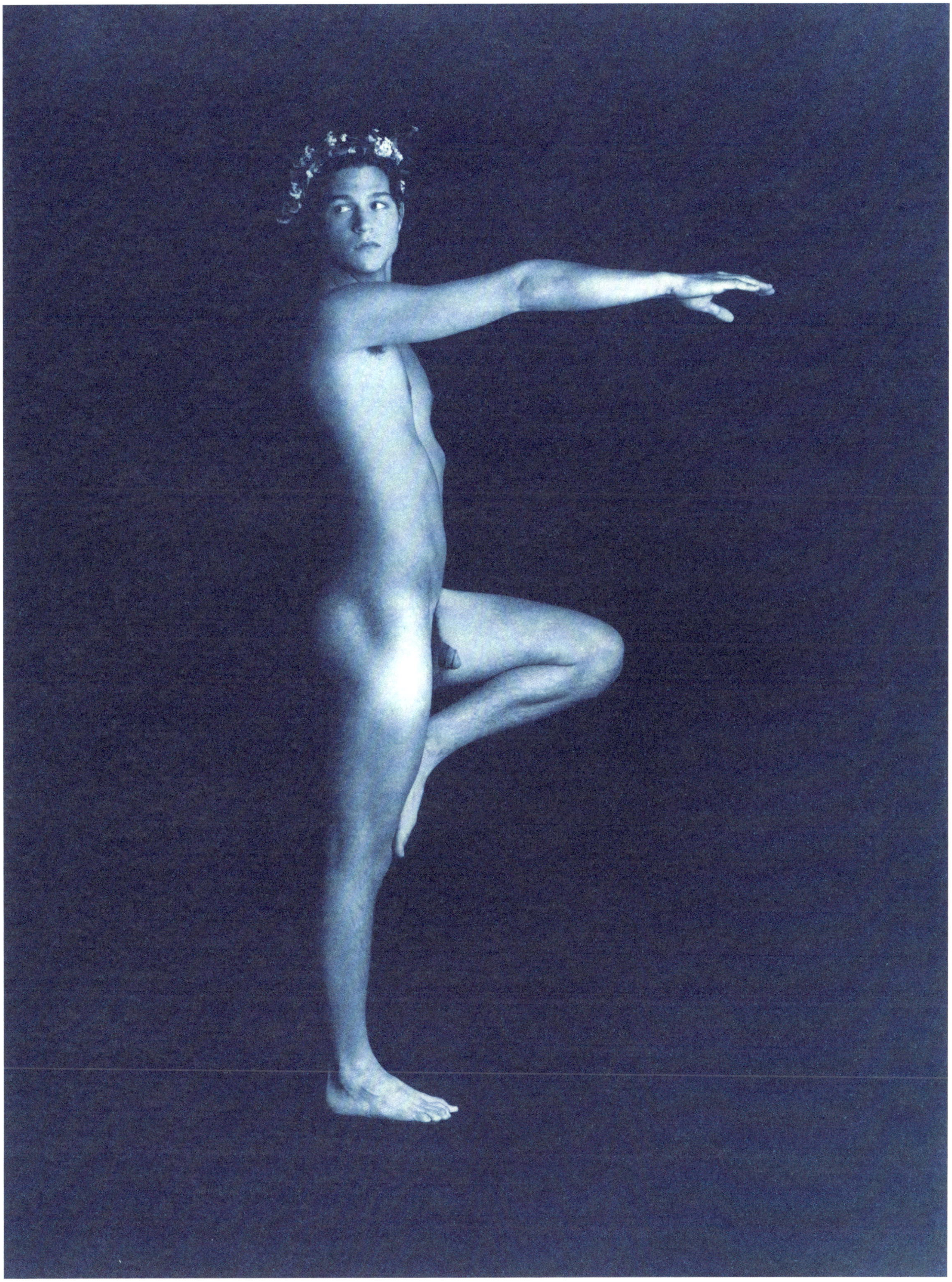

G

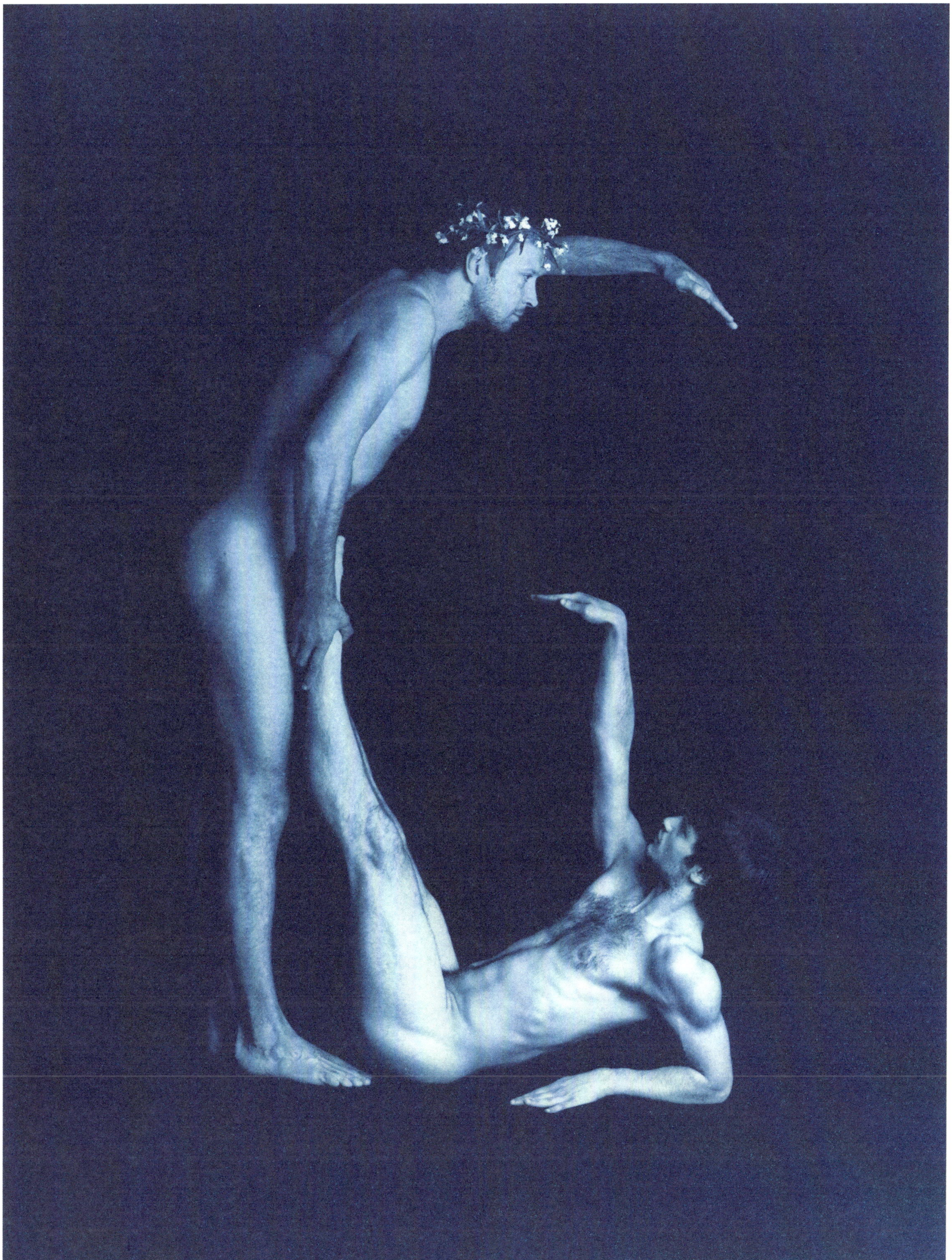

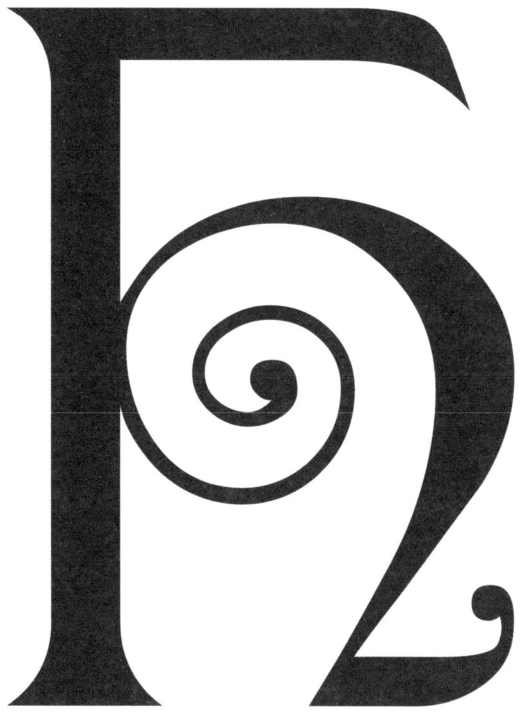

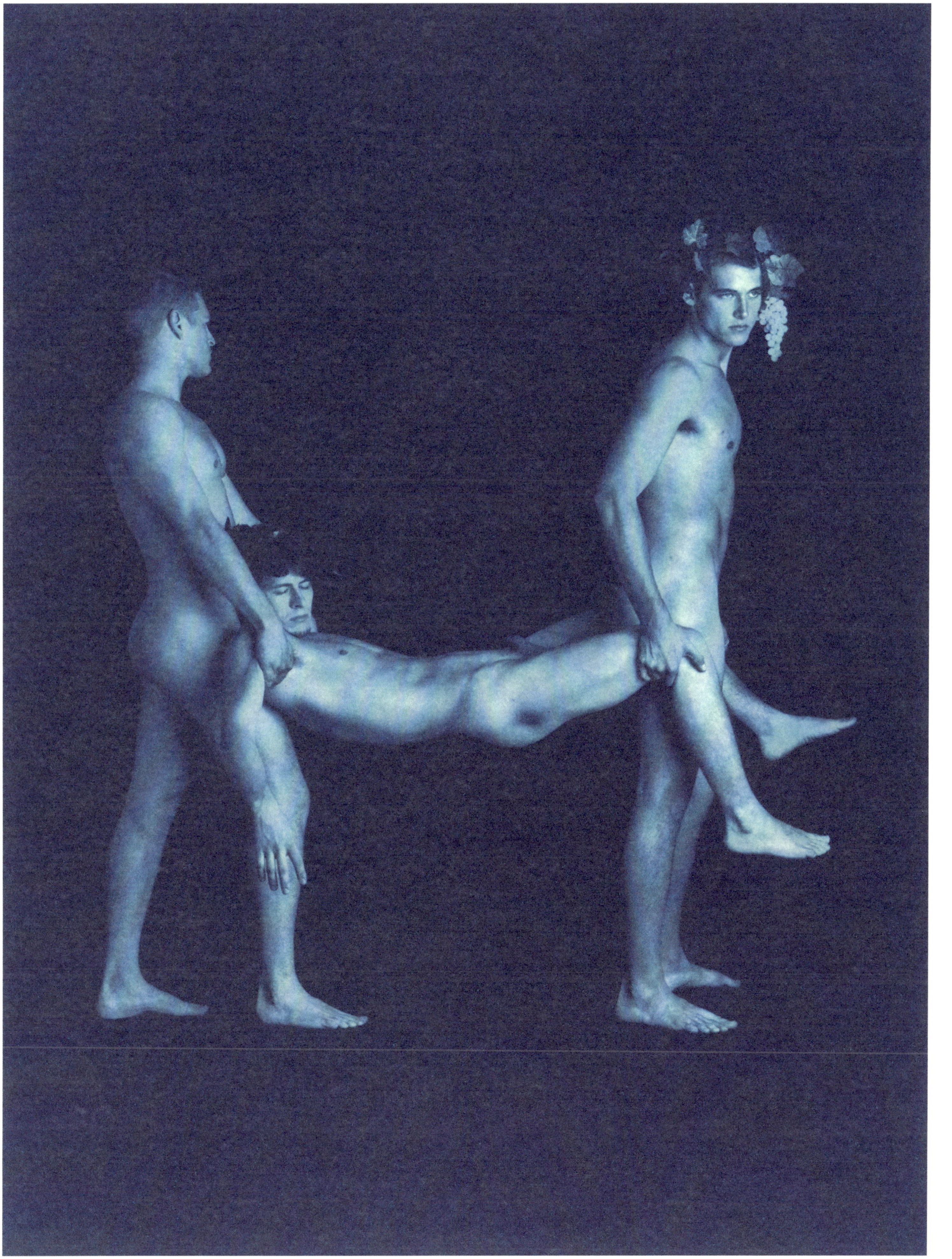

Г

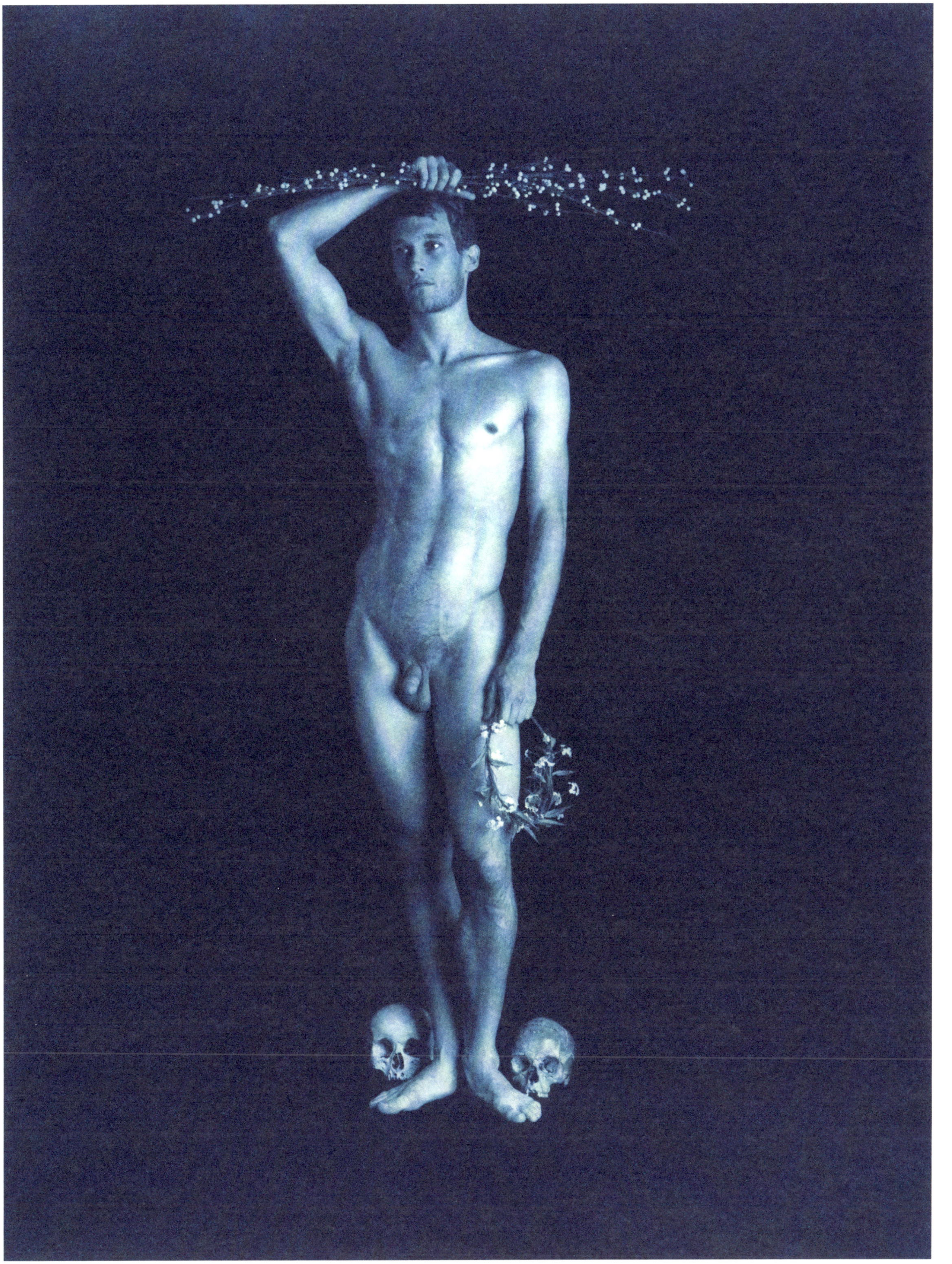

J

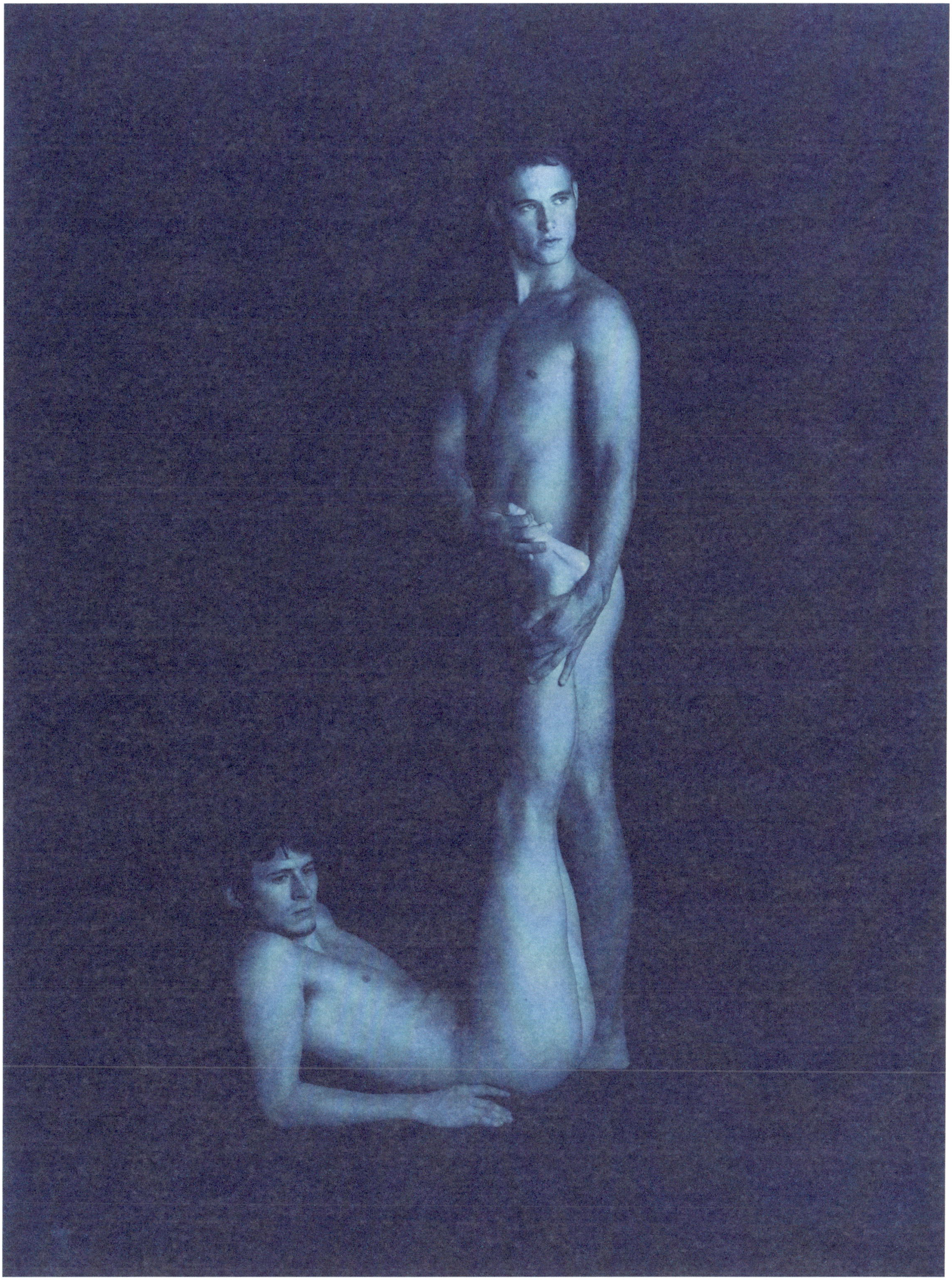

K

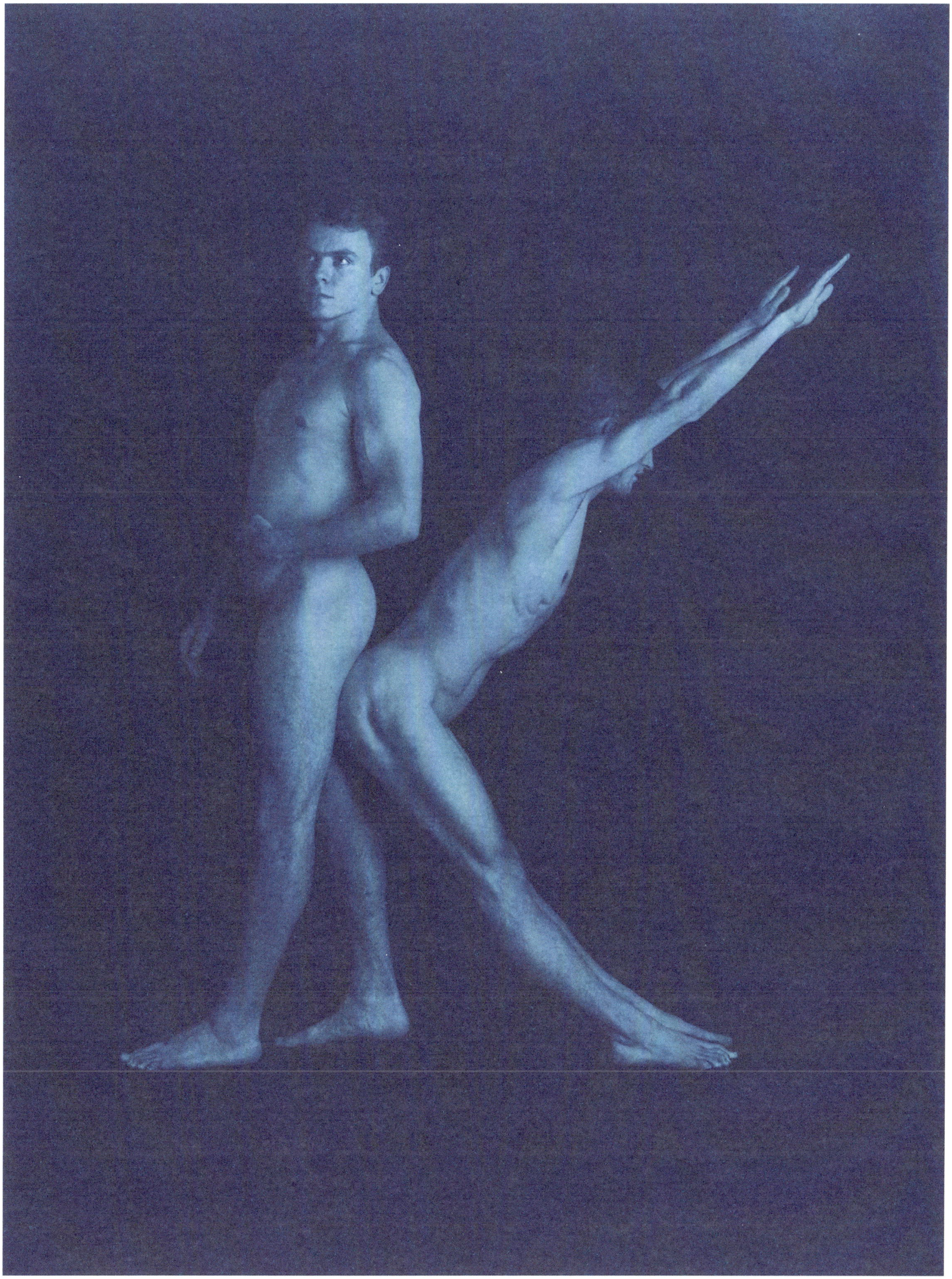

L

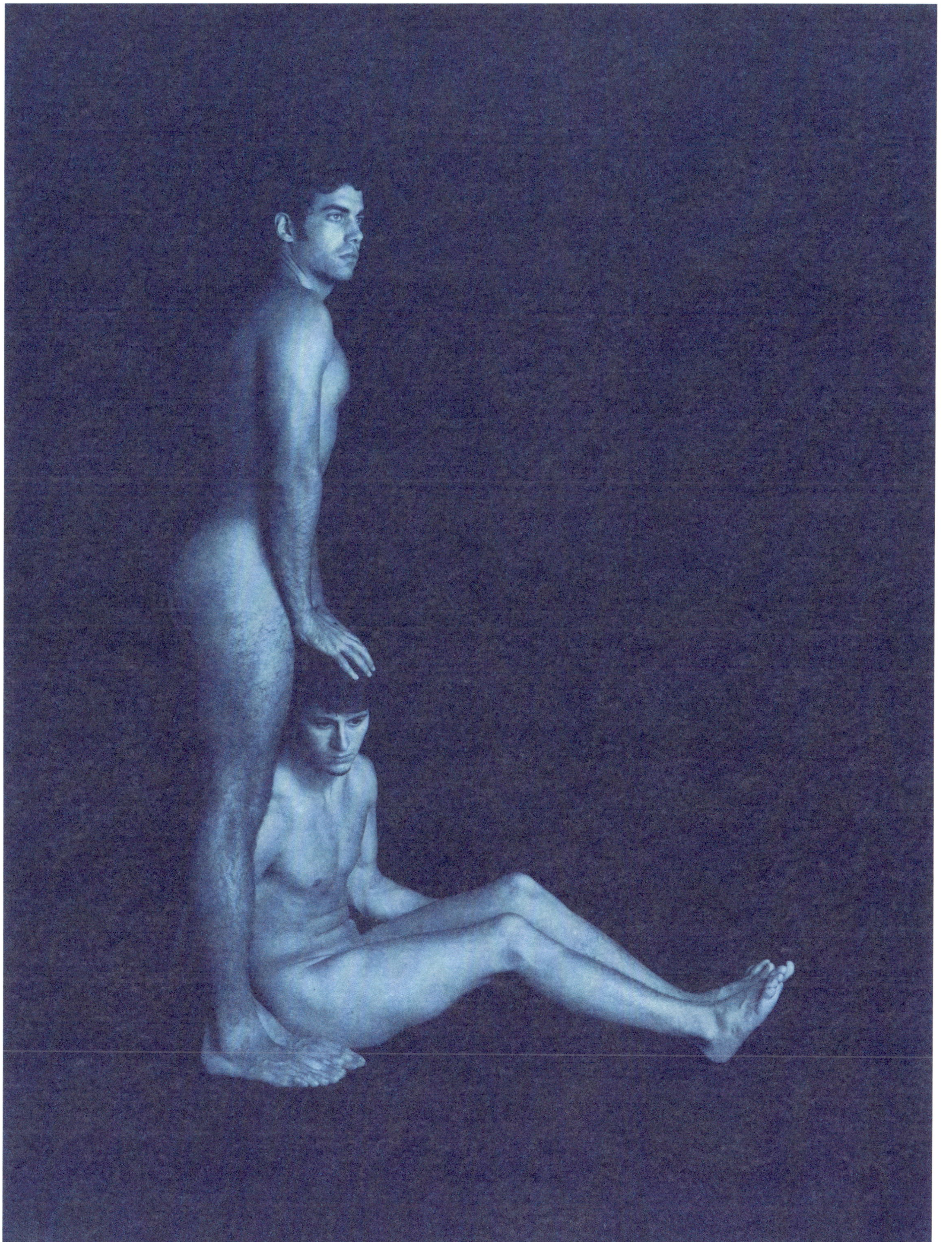

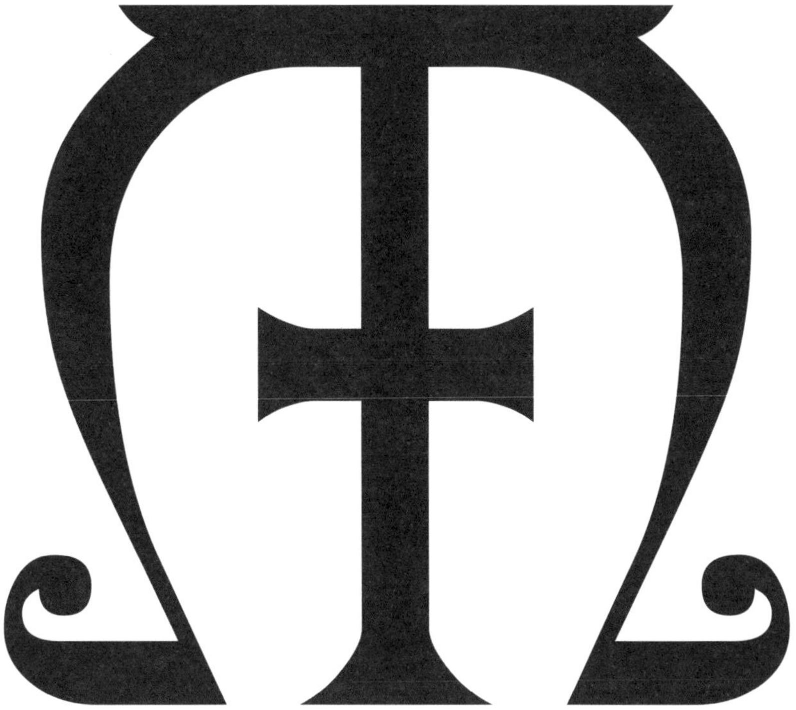

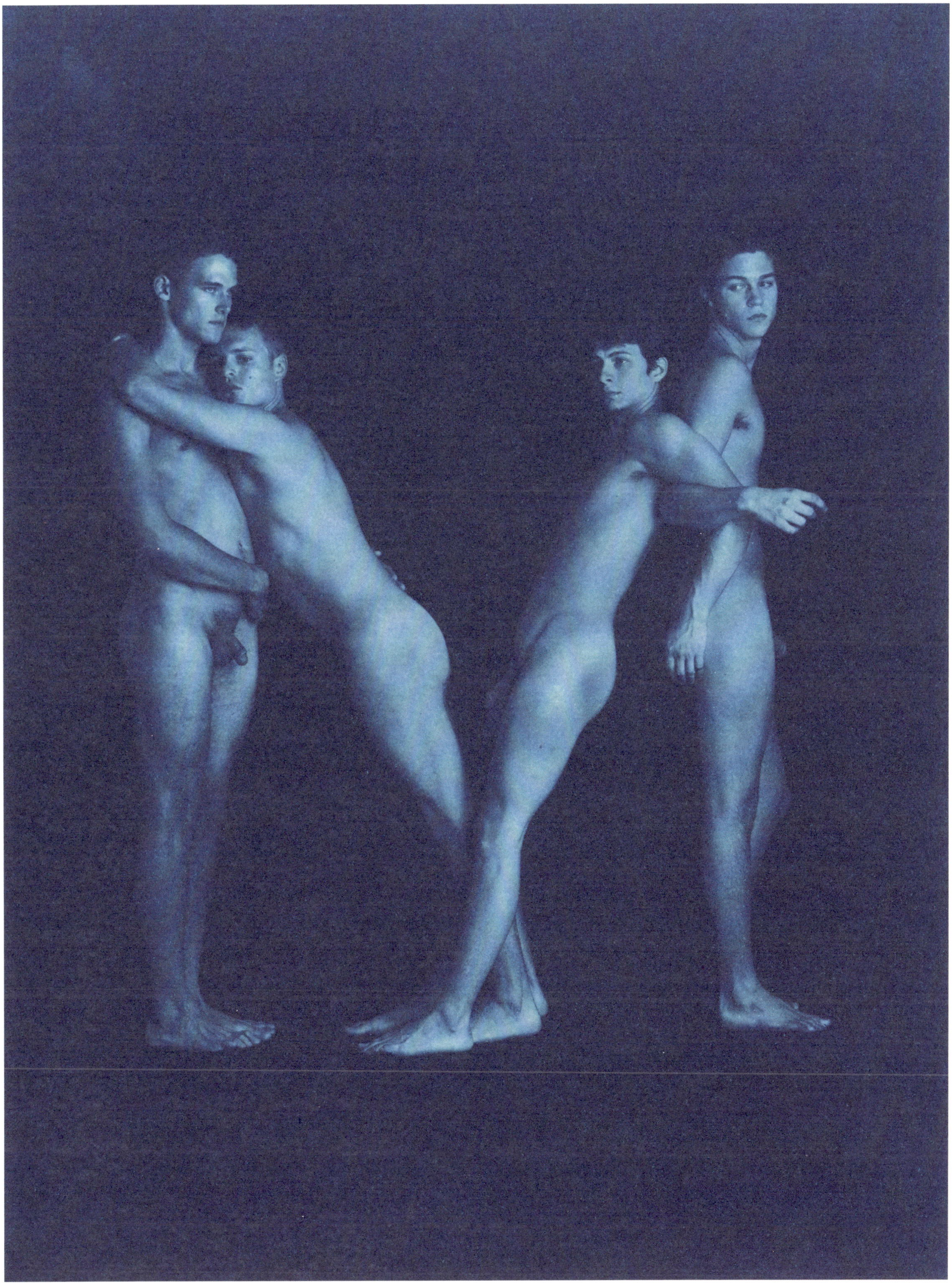

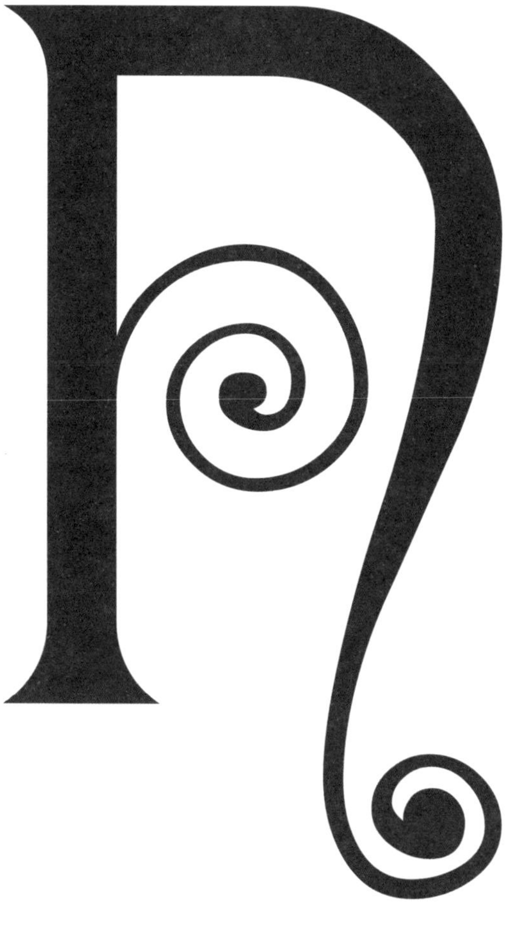

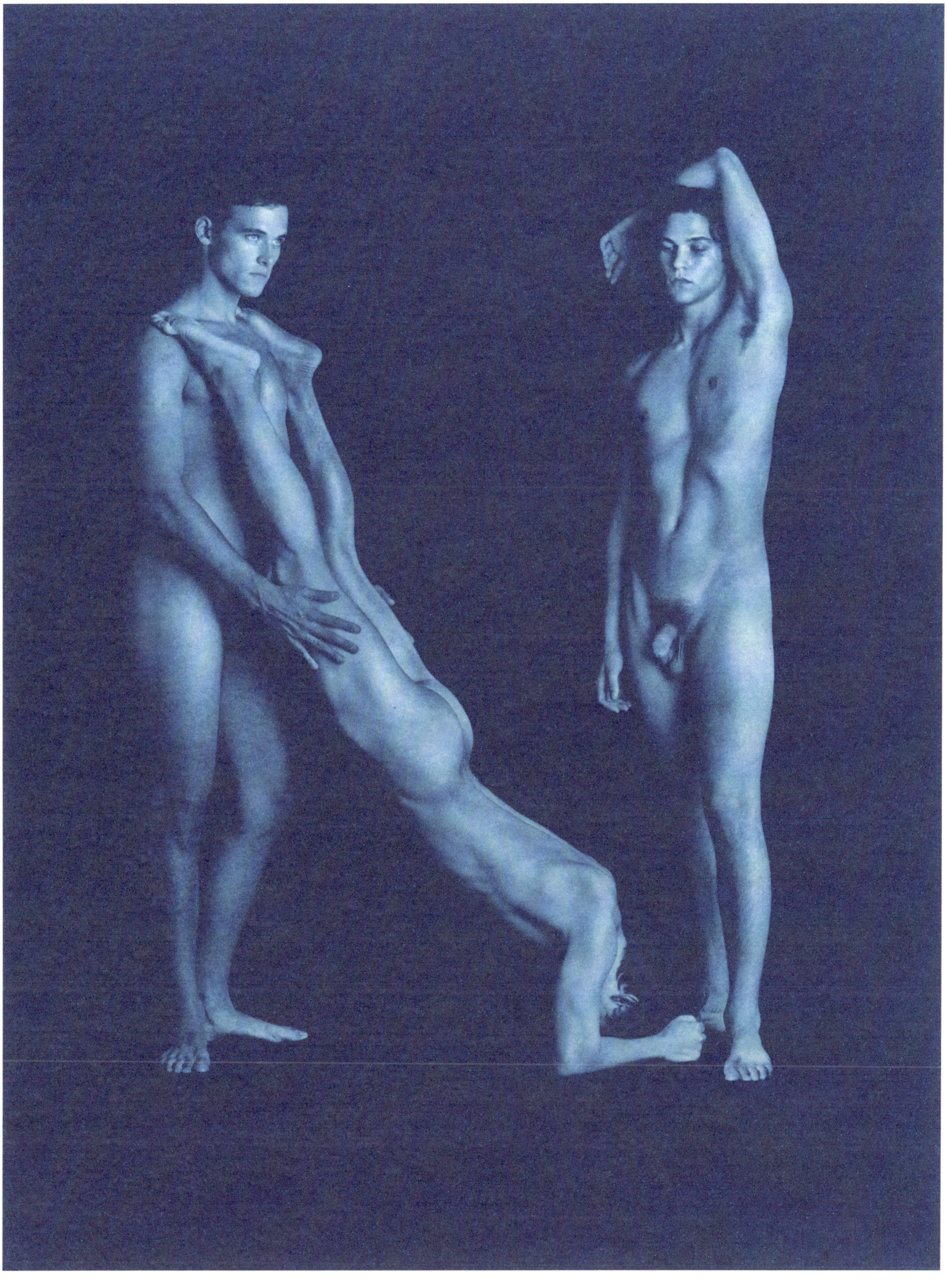

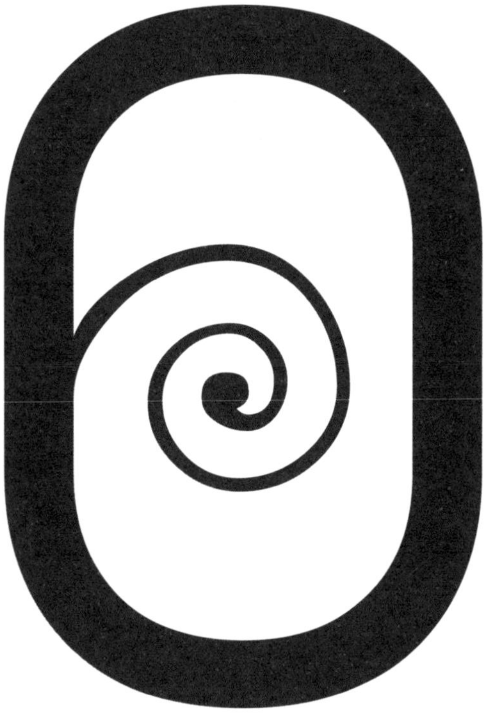

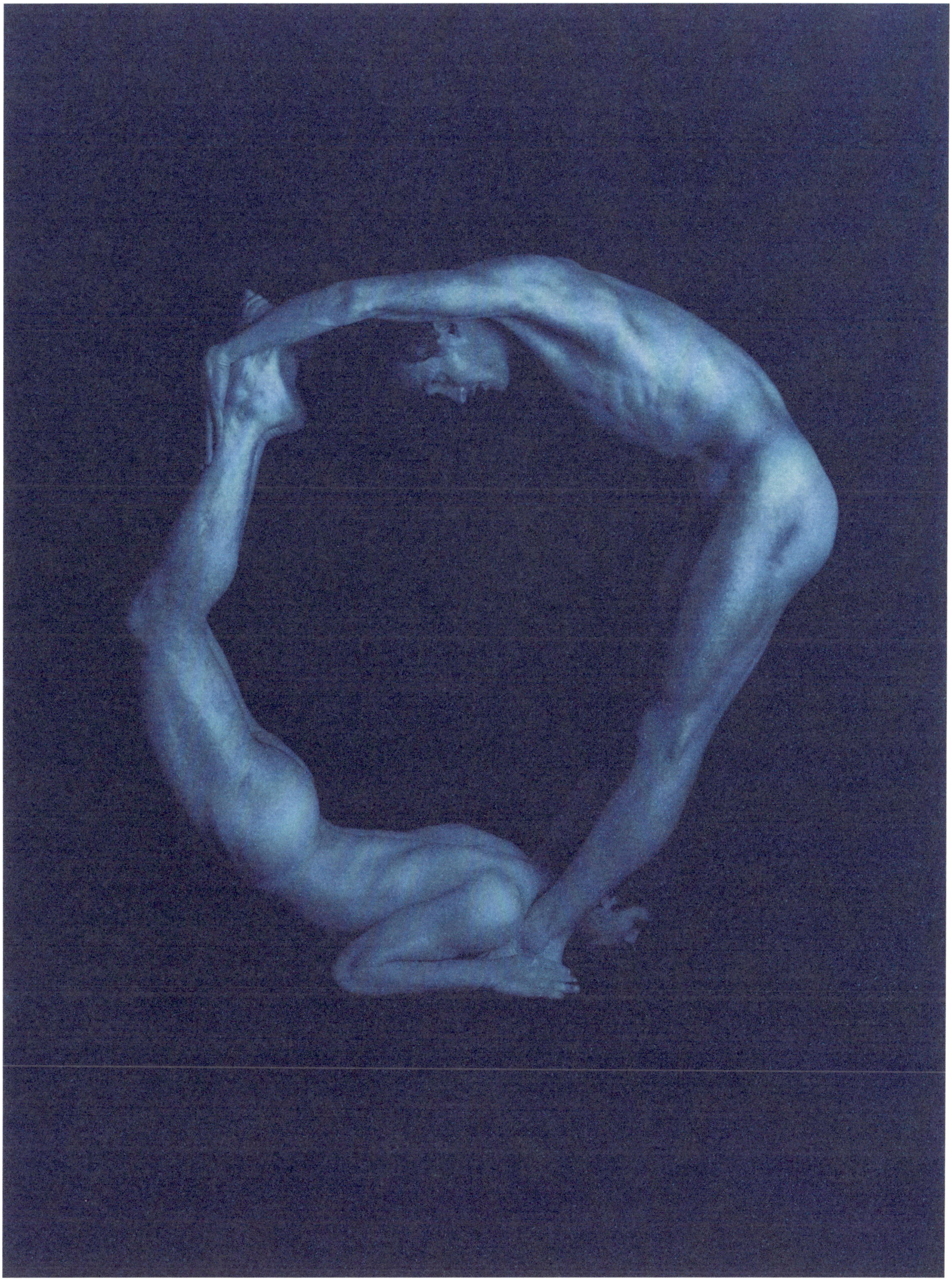

P

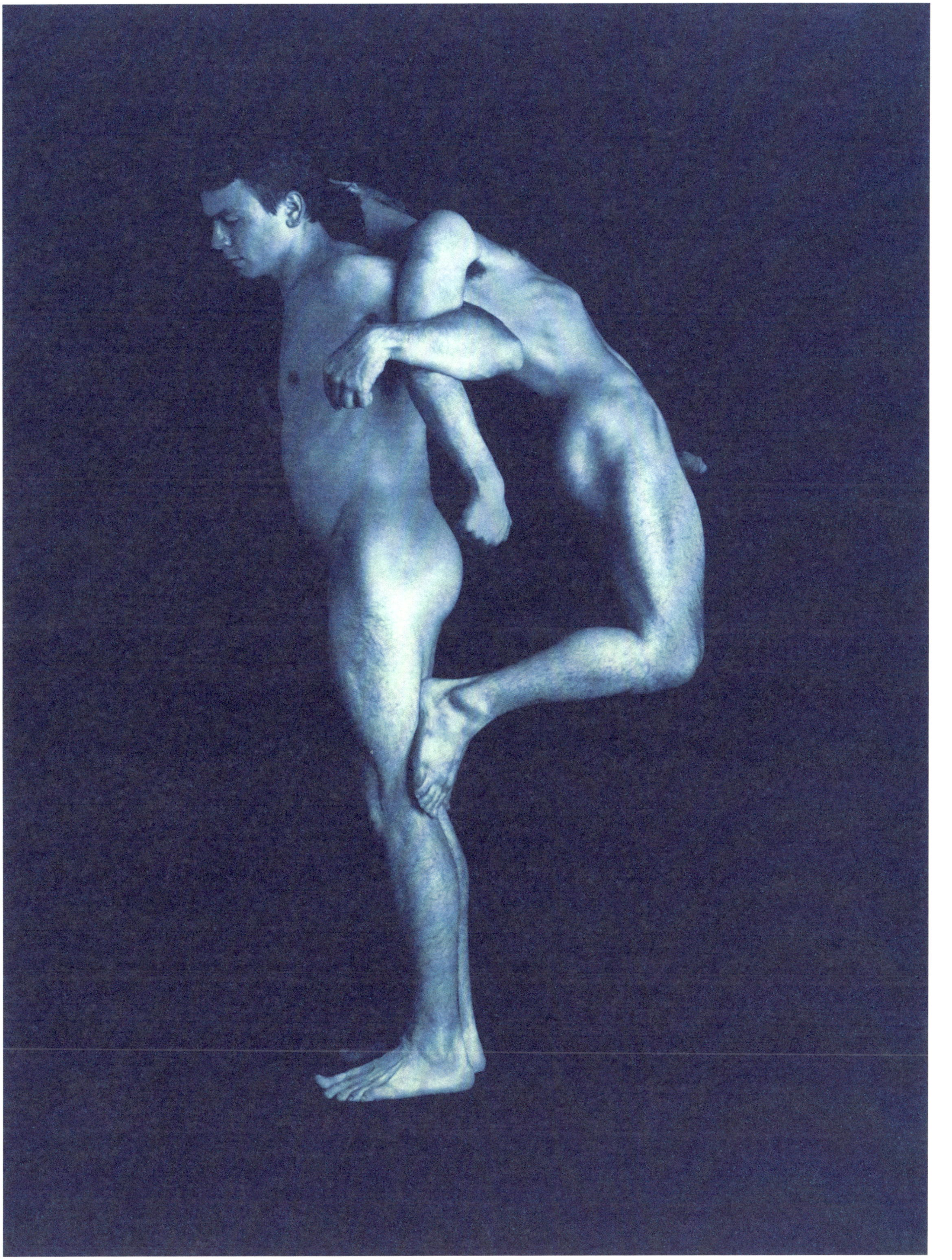

Q

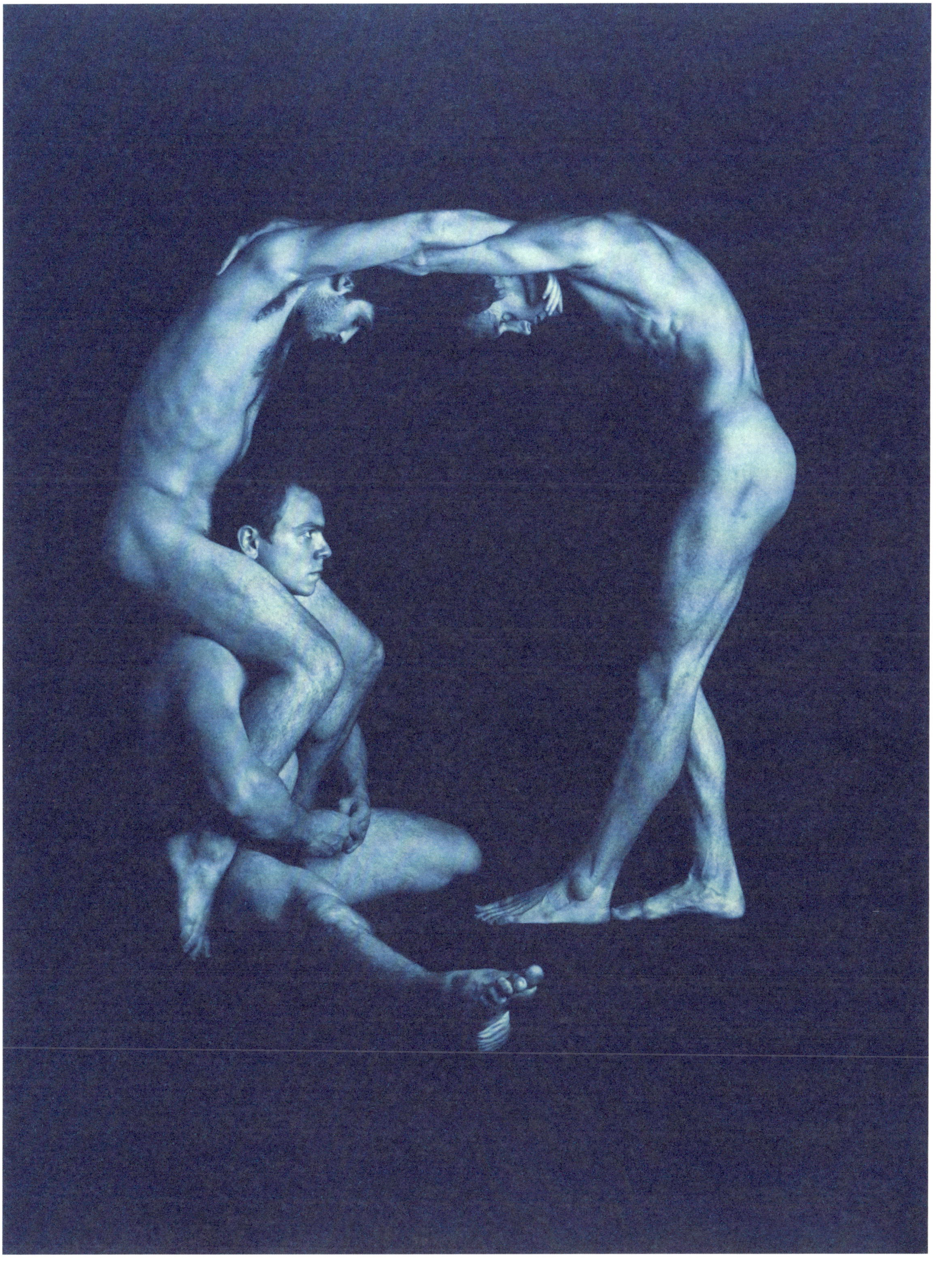

R

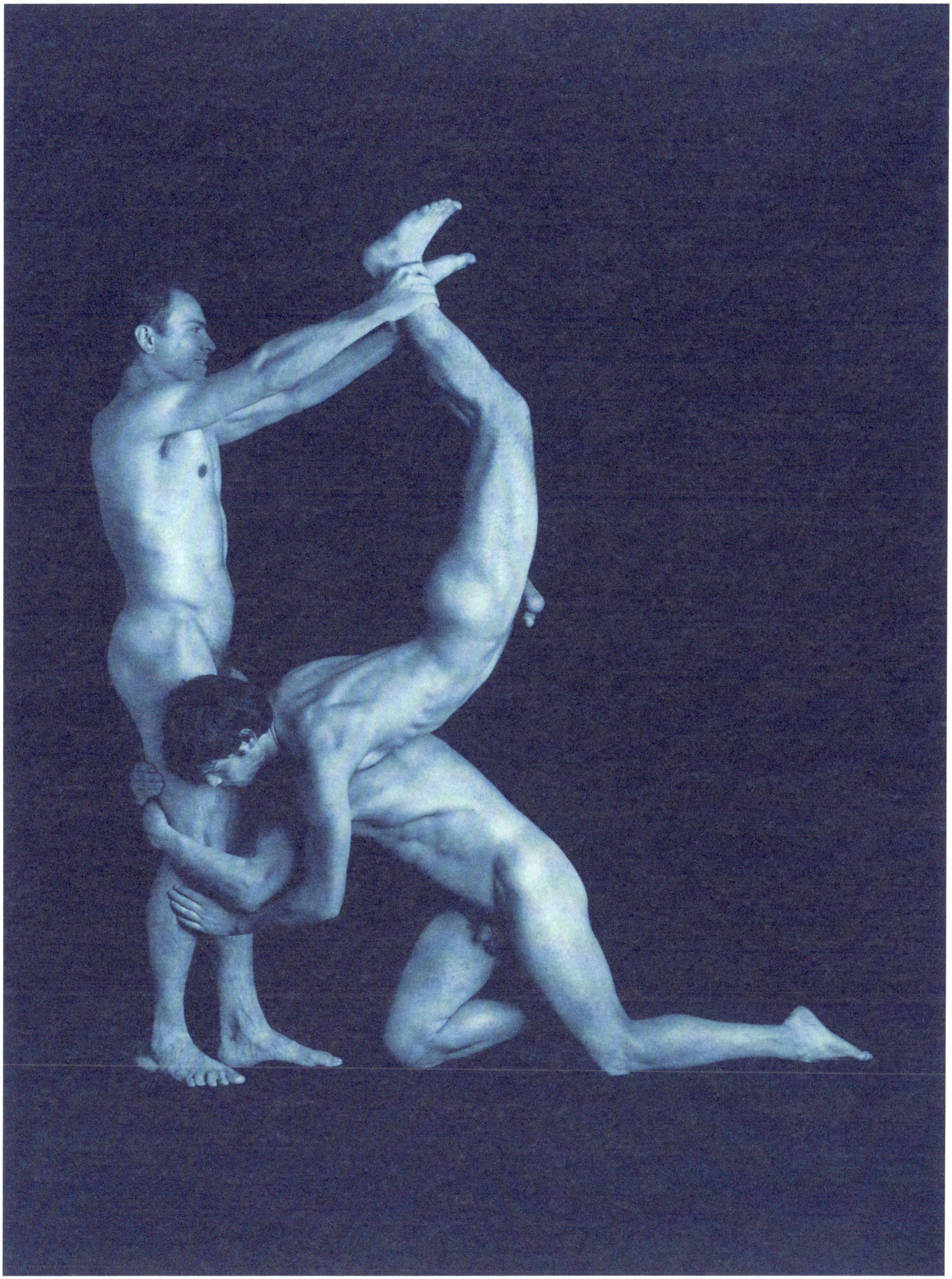

S

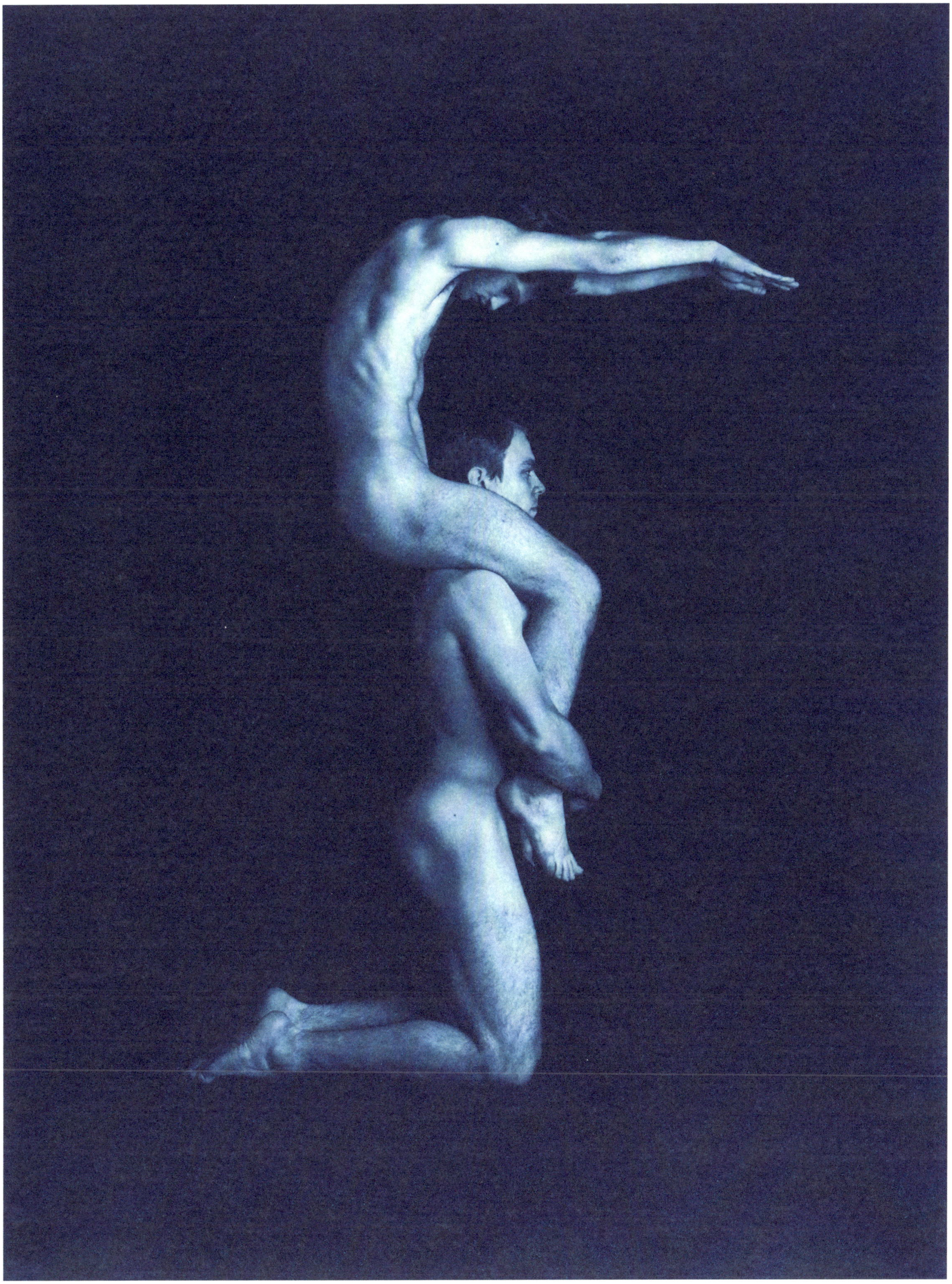

T

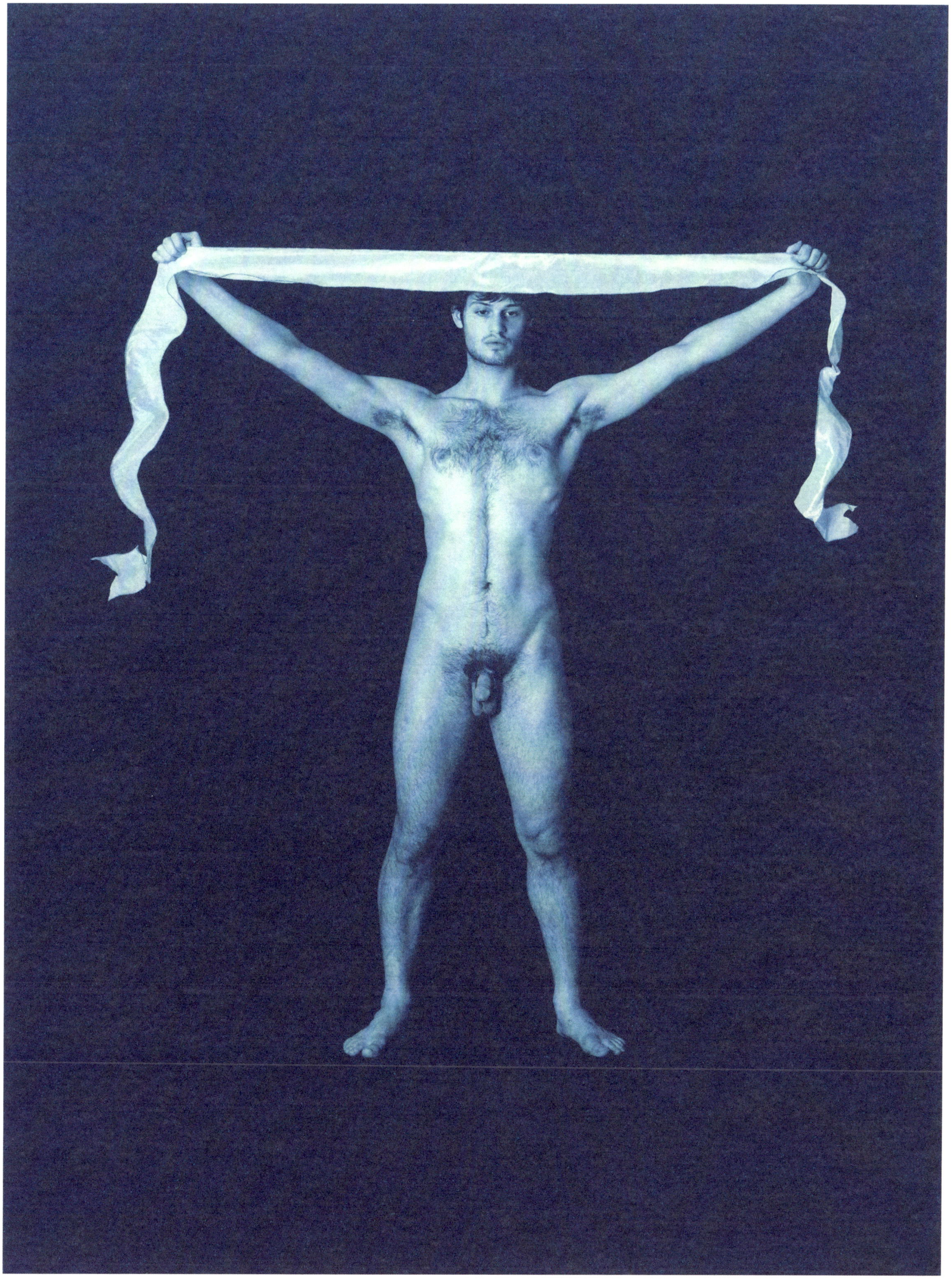

U

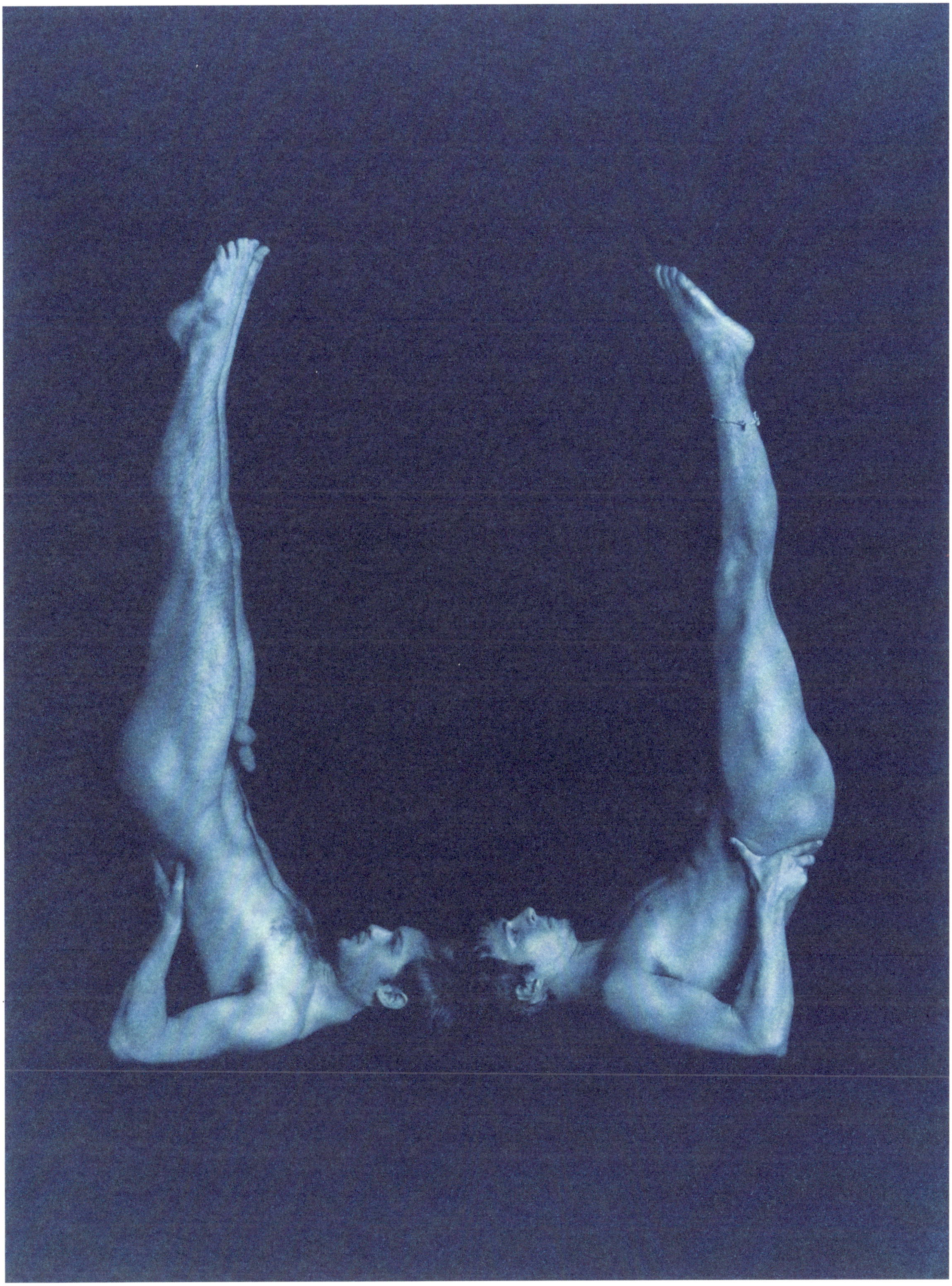

V

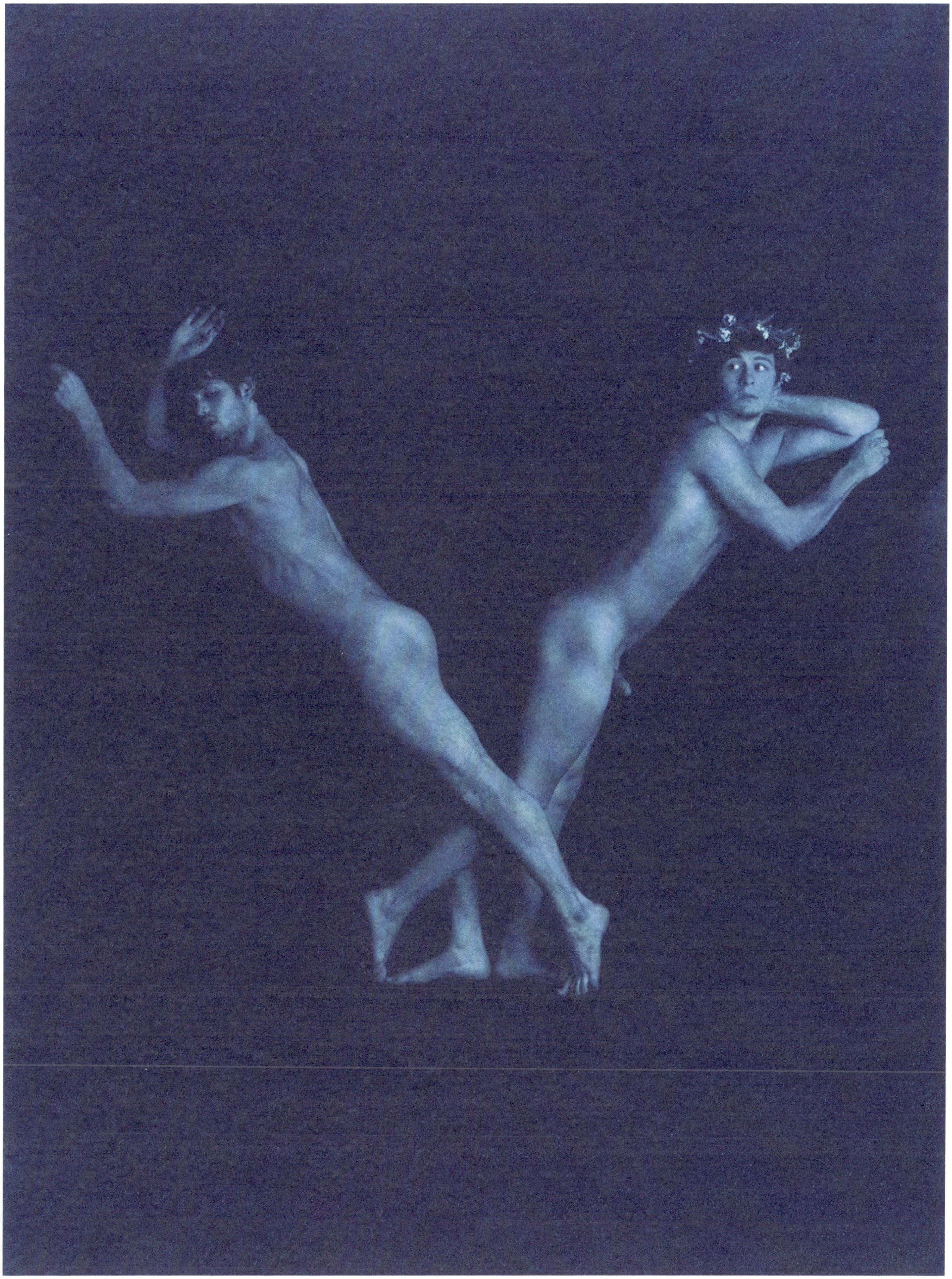

W

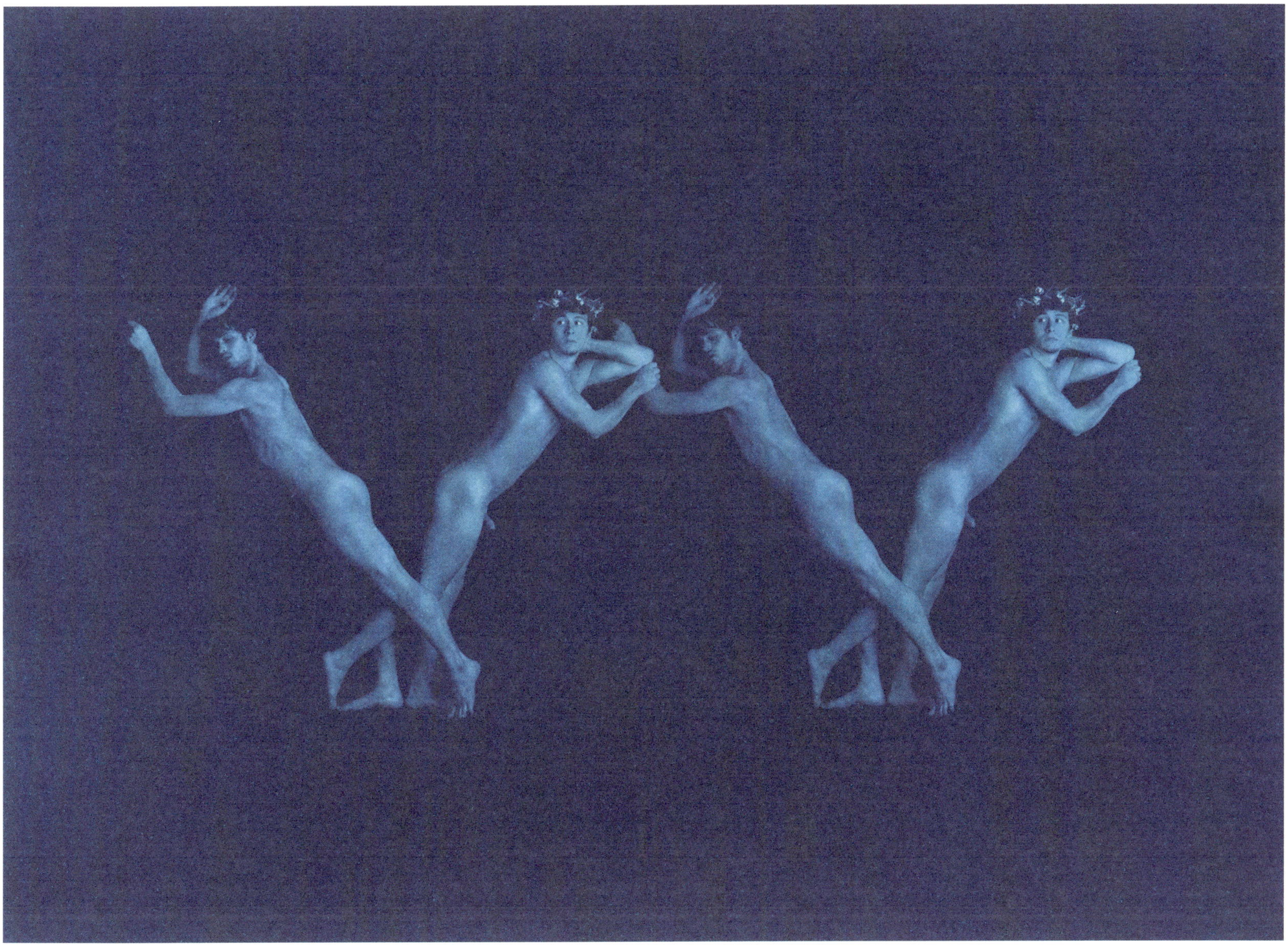

X

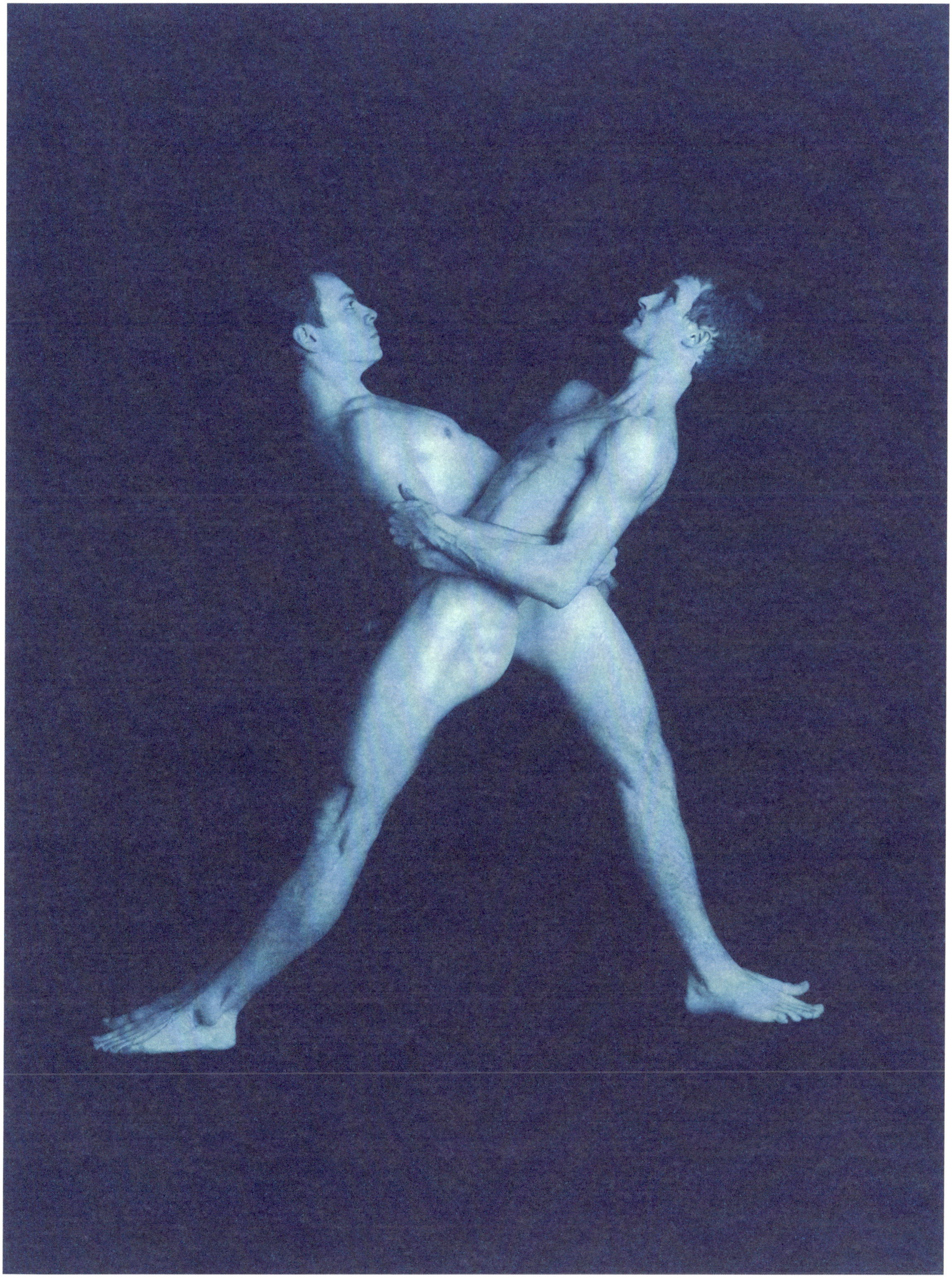

Y

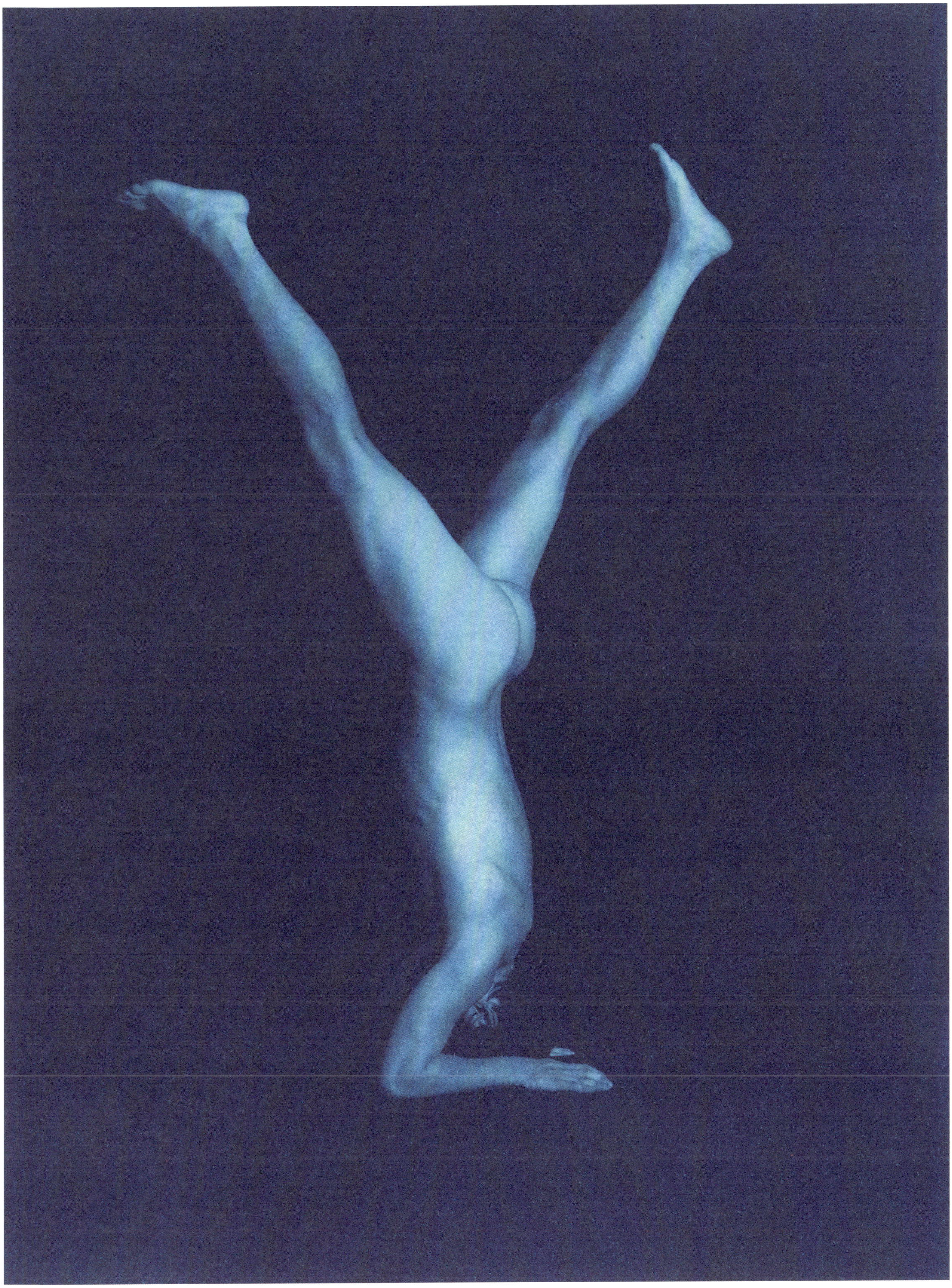

Z

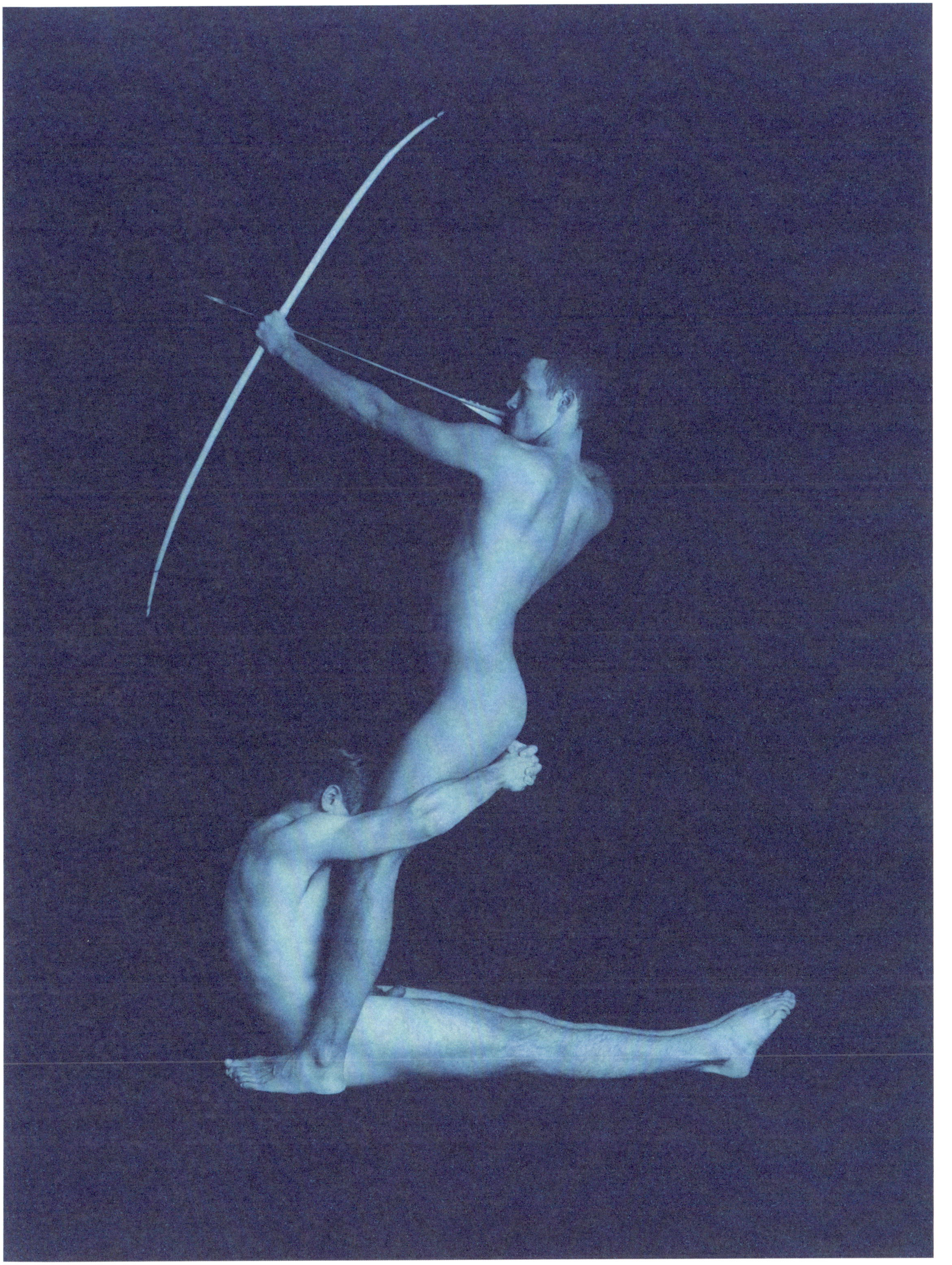

Alphabet
Peter McGough

Edition of 1,000

Cyanotype prints by
Kellyann Petry

ISBN 978-1-961883-06-2